Biggest and smallest

CONTENTS

Land mammals 2

Sea mammals 4

Birds. 6

Snakes 8

Frogs 10

Fish 12

Beetles 14

Index 16

Land mammals

African elephant

The *biggest* land animal is an African elephant.
A big male elephant may weigh more than 6 cars.
He eats many kinds of plants.

Savi's Pigmy shrew

The *smallest* animal with fur is a tiny shrew. Two of them weigh less than one penny. They feed on insects and grubs.

Sea mammals

Blue whale

The *biggest* animal in the world is the Blue whale. It may weigh more than 15 elephants. It feeds on small creatures, like shrimps.

Piebald dolphin

The *smallest* dolphin in the sea is the Piebald dolphin. It weighs less than a sheep.

Birds

Ostrich

The *biggest* of all birds is the ostrich. A big one could not get through a classroom door. It would have to bend down. The ostrich cannot fly but it can run very fast.

The *smallest* of all birds is a tiny humming bird. It is smaller than many butterflies. It feeds on nectar.

Humming bird

Snakes

The *biggest* of all snakes is the huge python. It could be as long as a classroom. It feeds on animals such as small goats, which it swallows whole.

Python

Thread snake

The *smallest* of all snakes is a thread snake.
It is shorter than a pencil.
It is thinner than the lead in a pencil.

Frogs

Goliath frog

The *biggest* of all frogs is the Goliath frog. It is as big as a melon. It feeds on small creatures.

One of the *smallest* of all frogs grows just over one centimetre long.

1 cm

Sooglossus gardineri

Fish

The whale shark is the *biggest* fish in the world. It may grow much longer than a classroom.

Whale shark

Dwarf pigmy goby

1 cm

The *smallest* fish is the Dwarf Pigmy goby.
It never grows longer than one centimetre.
Its body is nearly transparent.

Beetles

The *biggest* of all beetles is the Goliath beetle. It may weigh as much as an apple. It feeds on rotten fruit.

Goliath beetle

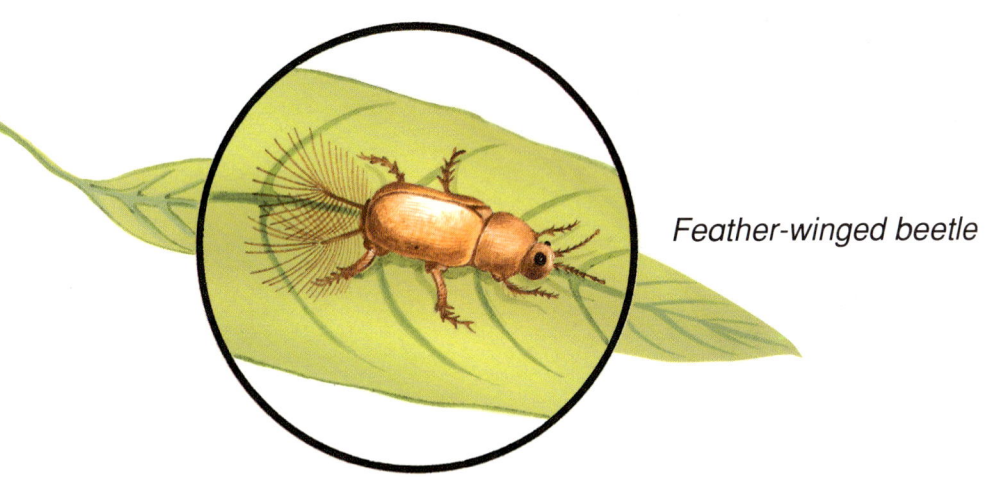

Feather-winged beetle

The *smallest* of all beetles is a feather-winged beetle. It is so small it could go through the eye of a needle.

Index

beetles 14, 15

birds 6, 7

fish 12, 13

frogs 10, 11

land mammals 2, 3

sea mammals 4, 5

snakes 8, 9